MISSOURI

The Show Me State

BY
JOHN HAMILTON

Abdo & Daughters

An imprint of Abdo Publishing | abdopublishing.com

abdopublishing.com

Published by ABDO Publishing, a division of ABDO, PO Box 398166, Minneapolis, Minnesota 55439. Copyright © 2017 by Abdo Consulting Group, Inc. International copyrights reserved in all countries. No part of this book may be reproduced in any form without written permission from the publisher. ABDO & Daughters™ is a trademark and logo of ABDO Publishing.

Printed in the United States of America, North Mankato, Minnesota.
032016
092016

Editor: Sue Hamilton   **Contributing Editor:** Bridget O'Brien
Graphic Design: Sue Hamilton
Cover Art Direction: Candice Keimig   **Cover Photo Selection:** Neil Klinepier
Cover Photo: iStock
Interior Images: AP, Corbis, Dreamstime, Ford Motor Company, Gateway Arch, Getty, Granger Collection, Gunter Kuchler, History in Full Color-Restoration/Colorization, Independence National Historical Park, iStock, Kansas City Chiefs, Kansas City International Airport, Kansas City Royals, Karl Bodmer, Kristy Henderson, L. Edward Fisher-Missouri Bankers Association, Library of Congress, Mile High Maps, Missouri Highway & Transportation Dept/USGS, Mountain High Maps, Museum of Finnish Architecture, National Weather Service, New York Historical Society, Olympic Games, One Mile Up, Ozark Living, Picture MO, Six Flags St. Louis, Sporting Kansas City, St. Louis Blues, St. Louis Cardinals, St. Louis Rams, St. Louis Star Times, St. Louis Zoo, Wikipedia.

Statistics: *State and City Populations*, U.S. Census Bureau, July 1, 2015/2014 estimates; *Land and Water Area*, U.S. Census Bureau, 2010 Census, MAF/TIGER database; *State Temperature Extremes*, NOAA National Climatic Data Center; *Climatology and Average Annual Precipitation*, NOAA National Climatic Data Center, 1980-2015 statewide averages; *State Highest and Lowest Points*, NOAA National Geodetic Survey.

Websites: To learn more about the United States, visit booklinks.abdopublishing.com. These links are routinely monitored and updated to provide the most current information available.

Cataloging-in-Publication Data

Names: Hamilton, John, 1959- author.
Title: Missouri / by John Hamilton.
Description: Minneapolis, MN : Abdo Publishing, [2017] | Series: The United
    States of America | Includes index.
Identifiers: LCCN 2015957618 | ISBN 9781680783278 (lib. bdg.) |
    ISBN 9781680774313 (ebook)
Subjects: LCSH: Missouri--Juvenile literature.
Classification: DDC 977.8--dc23
LC record available at http://lccn.loc.gov/2015957618

CONTENTS

THE SHOW ME STATE

I n the early 1800s, Missouri was the launching point for many explorers and settlers heading west. The Lewis and Clark Expedition began near St. Louis, Missouri. Today, St. Louis is called the "Gateway to the West." The city's Gateway Arch is the tallest monument in the United States.

Missouri is a land with Southern and Midwestern traditions all rolled into one. Banjos and square dancing compete with blues and indie rock bands. Kansas City barbecue is legendary, while St. Louis thin-crust pizza is unforgettably unique. Missouri is also filled with natural beauty, from the Northern Plains to the wooded Ozark Mountains in the south.

People from Missouri have a reputation of being skeptical until something is proven to them. In 1899, Missouri politician Willard Vandiver once said, "I'm from Missouri, and you have got to show me." That is why today Missouri is called "The Show Me State."

The Hodgson Water Mill is in Ozark County, Missouri. The mill once used the flowing water from Bryant Creek to grind grains.

The Gateway Arch in St. Louis, Missouri, is the tallest monument in the United States.

QUICK FACTS

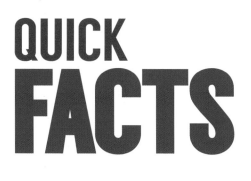

Name: Missouri is named after the Missouri River, which runs along the state's eastern border. The river and state are both named after a tribe of Native Americans called the Missouri.

State Capital: Jefferson City, population 43,132

Date of Statehood: August 10, 1821 (24th state)

Population: 6,083,672 (18th-most populous state)

Area (Total Land and Water): 69,707 square miles (180,540 sq km), 21st-largest state

Largest City: Kansas City, population 470,800

Nickname: The Show Me State

Motto: *Salus populi suprema lex esto* (The welfare of the people shall be the supreme law)

State Bird: Bluebird

White Hawthorn

State Flower: White Hawthorn Blossom

Galena

State Mineral: Galena

Flowering Dogwood

State Tree: Flowering Dogwood

State Song: "The Missouri Waltz"

Highest Point: Taum Sauk Mountain, 1,772 feet (540 m)

Taum Sauk Mountain

Lowest Point: St. Francis River, 230 feet (70 m)

Average July High Temperature: 89°F (32°C)

Record High Temperature: 118°F (48°C), in Union and Warsaw on July 14, 1954

St. Francis River

Average January Low Temperature: 21°F (-6°C)

Record Low Temperature: -40°F (-40°C), in Warsaw on February 13, 1905

Harry S. Truman

Average Annual Precipitation: 43 inches (109 cm)

Number of U.S. Senators: 2

Number of U.S. Representatives: 8

U.S. Presidents Born in Missouri: Harry S. Truman (33rd president)

U.S. Postal Service Abbreviation: MO

GEOGRAPHY

Missouri is in the Midwestern region of the United States. The Missouri River flows approximately west to east through the middle of the state. It divides Missouri into two large geographical parts. There are also two smaller additional regions.

North of the Missouri River are plains and gently rolling hills. This Northern Plains region is the result of ancient glaciers that scoured the land thousands of years ago. Ice sheets up to one-mile (1.6 km) thick bulldozed the land flat. When they melted, they left behind rich soil for farming.

The Osage Plains is a region in western Missouri, south of the Missouri River. It is part of America's North Central Plains. The land in the Osage Plains isn't as fertile as in the north.

Much of Missouri is flat plains or gently rolling hills.

IOWA

N

0 ——————— 100 miles
0 ——————— 100 km

NEBRASKA

ILLINOIS

Missouri River

Missouri River

Mississippi River

KANSAS

Kansas City

Jefferson City ★

MISSOURI

St. Louis

Springfield

OKLAHOMA

KENTUCKY

ARKANSAS

TENNESSEE

Missouri's total land and water area is
69,707 square miles (180,540 sq km).
It is the 21st-largest state. The state
capital is Jefferson City.

Regions of Missouri

Northern Plains

Osage Plains

Ozark Plateau

Bootheel

The Ozark Plateau is a large region south of the Missouri River. Also called the Ozark Mountains, this heavily forested area has many rough hills and deep valleys. There are also thousands of limestone caves in the region. The state's highest point is in the Ozark Plateau. It is Taum Sauk Mountain, which rises up 1,772 feet (540 m).

In the southeastern corner of Missouri is an irregularly shaped area called the Bootheel region. (It resembles the shape of a boot's heel.) It is part of the Mississippi River Delta. The land here is flat because of silt dropped by Mississippi River floods over thousands of years. The resulting soil is fertile for agriculture.

The New Madrid Earthquake Fault Zone is centered in the Bootheel region. A fault, or break in the Earth's crust, lies deep underground. When the ground suddenly shifts, it causes earthquakes. Thousands of small earthquakes have been recorded in the Bootheel region. Most are too small for people to feel, but scientists worry that a large earthquake could devastate unprepared residents.

The Mississippi River flows down the entire eastern border of Missouri. Many barges carry bulky cargo up and down the river. St. Louis, Missouri, is a major port along the Mississippi River.

The other big river in the state is the Missouri River. It makes up Missouri's northwestern border before turning east at Kansas City. From there, it generally flows eastward, eventually emptying into the Mississippi River near St. Louis.

Farmland spreads out from the Missouri River.

CLIMATE AND
WEATHER

Because it is near the center of North America, Missouri has a continental climate. In general, there are hot, humid summers and cold, snowy winters. Due to its southern location, winters are not usually as harsh as some other Midwestern states.

Missouri has many kinds of weather from day to day. Drafts of cold air from Canada sometimes blow over the state. Warm, humid air comes from the Gulf of Mexico. Missouri also experiences dry air blowing from the southwestern United States.

Missouri summers are usually hot and sticky. The average July high temperature is 89°F (32°C). The record high temperature occurred on July 14, 1954, in the towns of Union and Warsaw. On that day, the thermometer soared to 118°F (48°C).

A firefighter drinks to rehydrate and cool down after responding to a fire in St. Louis, Missouri, on a hot, humid July day.

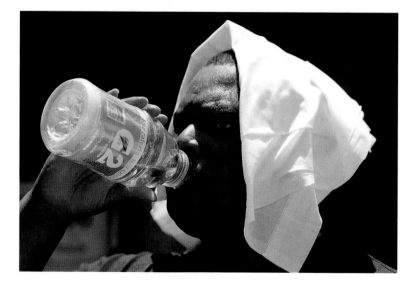

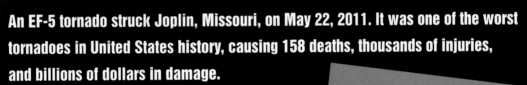

An EF-5 tornado struck Joplin, Missouri, on May 22, 2011. It was one of the worst tornadoes in United States history, causing 158 deaths, thousands of injuries, and billions of dollars in damage.

The average January low temperature in Missouri is 21°F (-6°C). The record low was a teeth-chattering -40°F (-40°C). It occurred on February 13, 1905, in the town of Warsaw.

Missouri is on the eastern edge of Tornado Alley, a region of the United States that sees the most tornadoes. On average, about 31 twisters strike Missouri each year.

CLIMATE AND WEATHER

PLANTS AND
ANIMALS

About 31 percent of Missouri is covered by forestland. That is roughly 14 million acres (5.7 million ha). About 85 percent of that is owned by private landowners. The majority of Missouri's forests are in the southern part of the state.

Common trees found in Missouri include oak, walnut, elm, hickory, pine, and red cedar. There is more rain in the southeastern part of the state. The damp soil supports bald cypress, oak, elm, and tupelo trees.

The Ozark Mountains of southern Missouri are famous for supporting many kinds of wildflowers. They bloom from spring until November. Many people like to drive down country roads spotting wildflowers.

The fire pink has sets of five bright-red petals. Another name for this flower is the scarlet catchfly, because it captures small insects with the sticky hairs on its stems. Its bright petals attract hummingbirds.

Fire Pink or Scarlet Catchfly

Other common wildflowers in the Ozarks include larkspur, purple coneflower, and columbine. Beautiful, but less common, wildflowers include showy lady's slipper, wild crocus, and forked aster.

A white-tailed deer stands in a forest in St. Louis County, Missouri.

An opossum mom carries her babies to a new location.

Before European-Americans settled Missouri, the state was home to many large mammals such as elk, bison, and bears. Trapping and hunting caused most of those animals to become extinct in the state. Conservation efforts have brought back small herds of elk and bison. Black bears are also spotted in southern Missouri.

Today, common animals seen living on the plains and in the forests of Missouri include white-tailed deer, coyotes, opossums, raccoons, rabbits, weasels, badgers, chipmunks, bats, and skunks. Squirrels are often seen scampering in the trees overhead. Minks, river otters, beavers, and muskrats can be found in many woods and wetlands. The official state animal is the Missouri mule. The offspring of horses and donkeys, these sturdy animals were prized by early settlers and farmers.

Many kinds of turtles, frogs, toads, lizards, salamanders, and snakes are found in Missouri. About 90 percent of the state's snakes are harmless. Venomous snakes that live in Missouri include copperheads, cottonmouths, western pygmy rattlesnakes, massasauga rattlesnakes, and timber rattlesnakes. Although dangerous, snakebites are rare. These reptiles play an important role in preying on rodent pests.

Birds often seen flying through the sky in Missouri include American robins, doves, crows, bald eagles, hawks, owls, cardinals, orioles, blackbirds, meadowlarks, and goldfinches. The official state bird is the bluebird.

The official state fish of Missouri is the channel catfish. It uses its cat-like whiskers to hunt for food. Other fish found in the state include bass, pike, carp, black crappie, trout, and sunfish.

The channel catfish is Missouri's official state fish.

HISTORY

P eople lived in today's Missouri long before the first European settlers arrived. Paleo-Indians were the ancestors of modern Native Americans. They migrated to Missouri 12,000 years ago, and perhaps much earlier. At first, they hunted animals and gathered plants. Eventually, they created settlements. Many built large earthen mounds for religious purposes such as burials.

By the 1600s, there were several Native American tribes living in Missouri. In the north and east were the Missouri and Illini people. They lived along the Grand and Missouri Rivers. In the south and west were the Quapaw and Osage people. Other tribes included the Otoe, Sauk, Ioway, Fox, Shawnee, and Delaware people. Almost all of the Native Americans were forced out of the state by white settlers by the 1830s.

Missouri (left) and Otoe (right) Native Americans were painted by the Western artist Karl Bodmer in the 1800s.

French hunters and miners began settling Missouri in the mid-1700s. Many arrived by boat, coming up the Mississippi River from New Orleans, Louisiana. Their first settlement was named Sainte Genevieve, along the west bank of the Mississippi River. Founded in 1735, it was located just south of present-day St. Louis, and was the first non-Native American settlement in Missouri. In 1764, St. Louis was founded. It began as a trading post and then grew as more settlers arrived.

Trappers and their pet cat travel down the Missouri River.

The Louis and Clark Expedition travels up the Missouri River in 1804.

In 1803, the United States bought a huge piece of land in the middle of the continent from France. It was called the Louisiana Purchase. (Today's state of Louisiana was just a small part of the area.) The sale almost doubled the land area of the United States. Missouri was part of the purchase.

President Thomas Jefferson wanted to find out what was in the new territory. He chose Meriwether Lewis and William Clark to lead an expedition called the Corps of

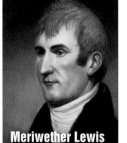

Meriwether Lewis

William Clark

Discovery. In 1804, they started at the mouth of the Missouri River near St. Louis. They traveled to the source of the river in today's Montana, climbed over mountains, and eventually arrived at the Pacific Ocean. In 1806, they returned to St. Louis, having lost only one man to sickness.

After the Lewis and Clark Expedition, St. Louis became an important launching spot for many expeditions and settlers. That is why today it is nicknamed the "Gateway to the West."

In 1812, Missouri Territory was formed. More settlers poured into the area. They wanted Missouri to become a state. Many were violently opposed to slavery. Other settlers, however, came from the South. They wanted to use slaves on their farms.

In 1821, Missouri was admitted to the Union as the 24th state. Because of a political agreement called the Missouri Compromise, it was allowed to be a slave state. However, future states west and north of Missouri would not be allowed to have slavery.

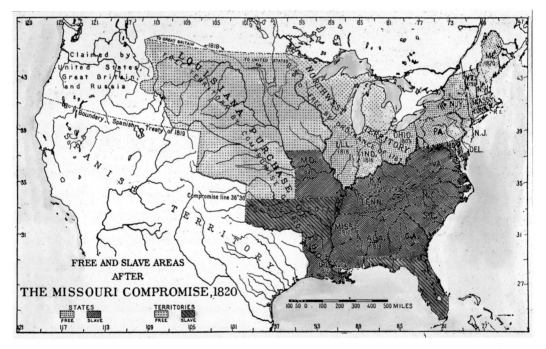

By the early 1820s, some states allowed slave labor, while other states made slavery illegal. One way to keep an uneasy peace in America was to make sure the number of slave states and free states remained about equal. When Maine and Missouri were considered for statehood, Congress agreed that Maine would join the Union as a free state in 1820, and Missouri as a slave state in 1821. This "Missouri Compromise" kept the balance equal.

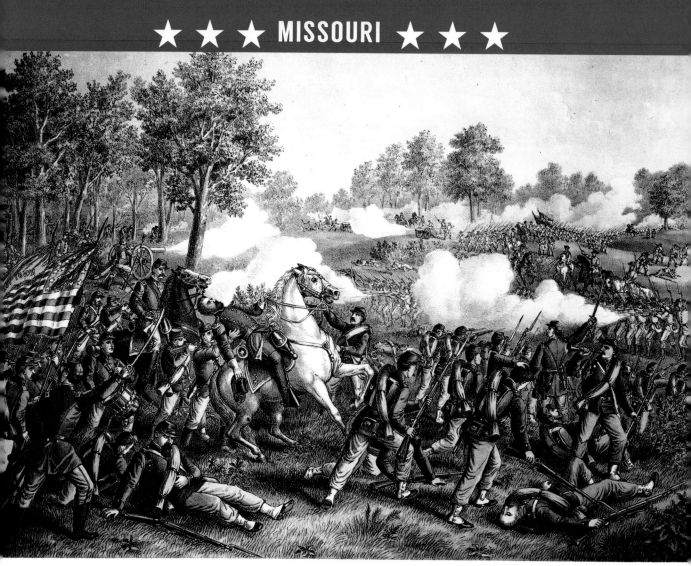

General Nathaniel Lyon was the first Union general to be killed during the Civil War. Lyon died in Missouri at the Battle of Wilson's Creek on August 10, 1861.

In 1861, the nation was plunged into the bloody Civil War (1861-1865). Missouri officially stayed in the Union rather than join the Southern Confederate States of America. However, many Missourians supported the South. About 30,000 fought for the Confederacy, while almost 110,000 fought for the Union. More than 1,200 battles were fought on Missouri soil. The Battle of Wilson's Creek in 1861 was the first major battle fought west of the Mississippi River. In 1865, the Union finally won the war, and the slaves were set free.

A Missouri farm family during the Great Depression.

Missouri prospered when America fought in World War I (1914-1918). The state's agricultural products were in high demand by overseas troops. However, when the Great Depression shattered America's economy starting in 1929, Missouri was hit hard. Banks failed, farms went bankrupt, and many people lost their jobs. Rural Missouri suffered greatly as the Depression caused hardships and poverty.

During World War II (1939-1945), Missouri recovered. Once again, the state's agricultural products were in high demand. More importantly, many new industries were built in Missouri. Kansas City became a major railroad hub and meatpacking center.

Today, Missouri's economy continues to grow. The state relies less on agriculture and more on industry and service businesses such as finance, retail, and tourism. St. Louis and Kansas City continue to expand as people leave rural areas and take advantage of opportunities in the cities and their suburbs.

DID YOU KNOW?

The New Madrid Earthquakes caused huge waves on the Mississippi River.

• In 1811 and 1812, one of the most violent series of earthquakes to ever strike the country happened in Missouri. Called the New Madrid Earthquakes, they shook the ground so violently that they were felt hundreds of miles away. They are named after the town of New Madrid, Missouri, in the state's Bootheel region, the epicenter of the destruction. The first quake happened on December 16, 1811. The following two quakes happened a few weeks apart, January 23 and February 7, 1812. The last earthquake was the strongest. Scientists estimate it measured 7.5 on the Richter scale. It caused the ground to rise and fall. Landslides buried many areas. Huge waves on the Mississippi River caused boats to wash ashore. Islands disappeared. Buildings collapsed. The quake was felt as far away as Washington, DC. Luckily, not many people were killed by the New Madrid Earthquakes because the region was so sparsely populated. However, if similar earthquakes were to occur today, they would cause much destruction and loss of life.

• Missouri is often nicknamed "The Cave State," thanks to its 6,400 caverns. That is more caves than any state except Tennessee. Most are in southern Missouri, in the Ozark Mountains region. They formed millions of years ago when rainwater seeped underground and slowly hollowed out tunnels in the limestone bedrock. The caves are home to such creatures as grotto salamanders and bats.

• In May 1804, the Lewis and Clark Expedition started near St. Louis, Missouri, and followed the Missouri River westward. The expedition nearly had a tragic beginning. Just a few days into the journey, Meriwether Lewis climbed a limestone cliff along the river. He slipped and almost fell 300 feet (91 m) to his death. As William Clark wrote in his trip diary, Lewis "Saved himself by the assistance of his Knife… he caught at 20 foot."

• Missouri's official state dessert is the ice cream cone. The frozen treat was first introduced at the 1904 World's Fair in St. Louis. The University of Missouri-Columbia has developed many ice cream products. Today, Missouri ranks 10th in ice cream production.

PEOPLE

George Washington Carver (c. 1864-1943) was one of the finest scientists in the United States. He was an inventor and botanist. He is most famous for his experiments in growing different kinds of crops. The son of a slave, Carver was born near Diamond, Missouri. He became an agricultural scientist in the late 1800s, and taught for almost half a century. When pests destroyed much of the cotton crop in the South in the late-1800s and early-1900s, he taught farmers to alternate planting new crops such as peanuts and soybeans. This "crop rotation" also replenished the soil. Carver invented many new uses for peanuts and sweet potatoes, which helped poor farmers sell more crops.

Harry S. Truman (1884-1972) was the 33rd president of the United States. He served as president from 1945-1953. He first took office during the final months of World War II. He made the difficult decision to drop two atomic bombs on Japan in 1945 in order to end the war. He also led the country during the Korean War (1950-1953) and the beginning of the Cold War. Truman was born in Lamar, Missouri.

Scott Joplin (c. 1867-1917) was a pianist and composer. He is most famous for ragtime music. He was born in Texas, but lived for many years in the cities of Sedalia and St. Louis, Missouri. Ragtime was a common kind of music played in the late-1800s and early-1900s. Joplin was a master of the style, and one of the best piano players in the world. His first big hit was "Maple Leaf Rag." He also composed jazz and big band swing music.

Samuel Clemens (1835-1910) was a writer and humorist. He is better known today as Mark Twain, which is how he signed his books. He was born in the town of Florida, Missouri, but was raised in Hannibal, Missouri. The Mississippi River town inspired the setting of Clemens's most famous novels, *The*

Adventures of Tom Sawyer, and *Adventures of Huckleberry Finn*. Both books tackle social issues, such as racism and morality, by using humor in a thoughtful way. Clemens was skilled at observing the good and bad things that happen in the world. In addition to writing novels, Clemens was a steamboat pilot, a miner, and a journalist.

Yogi Berra (1925-2015) was one of Major League Baseball's greatest catchers. He is best remembered for his many years playing for the New York Yankees from 1946-1963. As a player, his teams won 10 World Series championships. He won the American League Most Valuable Player Award three times. He was beloved for his silly "Yogi-isms," such as "It ain't over 'til it's over." Berra was born and grew up in St. Louis, Missouri.

Maya Angelou (1928-2014) was one of America's most acclaimed authors and poets. Also a civil rights activist, her writing often dealt with African American culture, racism, and family. Her book of poetry *Just Give Me a Cool Drink of Water 'fore I Diiie* was nominated for a Pulitzer Prize, writing's highest honor. Her most-loved book is her first autobiography, *I Know Why the Caged Bird Sings*. Angelou was born in St. Louis, Missouri.

CITIES

Kansas City is the largest city in Missouri. Its population is 470,800. Together with its suburbs and surrounding communities, the metropolitan area is home to almost 3 million people. The city is located where the Missouri and Kansas Rivers meet. Across the Missouri River is its smaller sister city, Kansas City, Kansas. They are named for the Kansa, a Native American tribe. In the late 1800s, the city became an important railway hub. Stockyards and factories spurred rapid growth. Today, Kansas City is a major center for finance and industry. Tourism is also important to the city's economy. Kansas City is famous for its museums, architecture, fountains, shopping, music, and barbecue cooking.

St. Louis is the second-largest city in Missouri. Its population is 317,419, but the larger metropolitan area contains almost 3 million people. St. Louis is located in the east-central part of the state, on the west bank of the Mississippi River. It was founded in 1764 by French fur trappers. The population began growing rapidly when steamships first arrived in the early 1800s. In 1904, the city hosted the World's Fair and the Summer Olympic Games. Today, St. Louis is a major manufacturing center. It is also home to several universities. The famous 630-foot (192-m) -tall Gateway Arch soars above the banks of the Mississippi River near downtown.

Jefferson City is the capital of Missouri. Located along the south bank of the Missouri River in the center of the state, its population is 43,132. It is named after President Thomas Jefferson. It became the state capital in 1826, although it had previously been a trading post for quite a few years. Today, the city has many manufacturing businesses. It is also a trade center for farm crops grown in the surrounding countryside. Top employers include state government, health care, education, and finance. The city is home to Lincoln University. The lovely state capitol building dominates Jefferson City's skyline. With an exterior made of Missouri marble, its dome rises 238 feet (73 m) and overlooks the Missouri River.

Springfield is the third-largest city in Missouri. Its population is 165,378. Located in southwestern Missouri in the Ozark Plateau region, the city was first settled in the early 1830s. It became a crossroads city when a railway line between St. Louis, Missouri, and San Francisco, California, was built that went through Springfield. The railway brought many people and jobs. Today, the biggest employers are health care, retail, manufacturing, and education. The city is home to Missouri State University. Tourism is also important. Springfield is just 44 miles (71 km) north of the city of Branson, a popular entertainment center featuring many live country music acts.

TRANSPORTATION

Missouri has 131,900 miles (212,272 km) of public roadways. One of the state's main highways is Interstate I-70. It stretches east and west across the middle of Missouri, from Kansas City to St. Louis. I-44 travels southwest from St. Louis, through Springfield, and into Oklahoma. I-55 follows the Mississippi River south from St. Louis to the Arkansas state line. I-35 cuts across the northwestern part of the state, entering from the Iowa border and exiting through Kansas City into the state of Kansas.

Both the Mississippi and Missouri Rivers are used by barges to haul bulky cargo such as grain. St. Louis is an important port along the Mississippi River.

A barge moves goods on the Mississippi River.

More than 10 million people travel through the Kansas City International Airport each year. It is one of Missouri's busiest airports.

Missouri has 17 freight railroad companies that haul material on 3,957 miles (6,368 km) of track. The most common goods hauled by rail include coal, farm products, cement, and chemicals. Amtrak has several passenger lines that connect Kansas City, Jefferson City, St. Louis, and other cities across the state.

Missouri's two biggest airports are Lambert-St. Louis International Airport and Kansas City International Airport. Southwestern Missouri is served by Springfield-Branson National Airport.

NATURAL
RESOURCES

Agriculture is not as big in Missouri as it once was, but it is still an important part of the state's economy. There are about 97,100 farms in the state. Combined, they occupy 28.3 million acres (11.5 million ha) of land. Most of the farms are in the fertile Northern Plains and southeastern Bootheel regions. The most valuable crops grown in Missouri include soybeans, corn, hay, sorghum, and wheat. Cotton and rice are grown mainly in the Bootheel region. Beef cattle, hogs, and turkeys are Missouri's most valuable livestock products.

Narragansett turkeys roam at a farm near Trimble, Missouri.

A Missouri logger secures a load of harvested Ozark timber onto a truck.

Thanks to its heavily wooded Ozark Mountains region, Missouri has almost twice the forestland of Iowa, Illinois, Kansas, and Nebraska combined. The wood and paper products industry employs about 28,000 people in the state and contributes nearly $1.7 billion to the economy.

In the past, mining was a major part of Missouri's economy. Today, it is no longer as important. The state continues to be the nation's leading supplier of lead, which is used to make car batteries and bullets. Other products mined in Missouri include zinc, crushed stone, and lime.

NATURAL RESOURCES

INDUSTRY

The service industry represents slightly more than half of Missouri's economy. Instead of manufacturing products, service industries sell services to businesses and consumers. It includes businesses such as advertising, financial services, health care, insurance, restaurants, retail stores, law, marketing, and tourism.

Vacationers spend nearly $11 billion in Missouri each year at tourism-related businesses. The tourism industry employs more than 280,000 Missourians. People flock to Missouri to enjoy music festivals, theaters, fine dining, museums, the beautiful Ozark Mountains, and the many activities available in Kansas City and St. Louis.

Visitors enjoy a riverboat ride down the Mississippi River.

Ford's Kansas City Assembly Plant builds F-150 trucks.

Manufacturing and transportation are very important to Missouri's economy. The state is home to more than 6,400 manufacturing firms, which employ more than 255,000 workers. Most of the businesses are in the Kansas City and St. Louis metropolitan areas. Top items made by Missouri manufacturers include transportation equipment, food processing, fabricated metal, machinery, chemicals, plastics, printing, computers, and electronics.

Both Ford and General Motors have large assembly factories in Missouri. Ford pickup trucks are made in the Kansas City area, while General Motors has an assembly plant near St. Louis. There are several aircraft manufacturers in the state, including Boeing, which makes military aircraft in the St. Louis area. Greeting card maker Hallmark Cards is based near Kansas City.

SPORTS

Missouri has several professional major league sports teams. The St. Louis Cardinals and the Kansas City Royals are both Major League Baseball teams. The Cardinals have won 11 World Series championships, while the Royals have won twice.

The Kansas City Chiefs play in the National Football League. They have won one Super Bowl championship, in 1970.

The St. Louis Blues skate in the National Hockey League. They are named after a song called "Saint Louis Blues." The team has won nine division titles, but never the Stanley Cup championship.

Sporting Kansas City is a professional soccer team. It has represented Kansas City, Missouri, since 1996, even though it plays home games at a stadium in Kansas City, Kansas.

Anglers fish for trout at Bennett Spring State Park near Lebanon, Missouri.

Outdoor sports are very popular in Missouri. There are 88 state parks, as well as many historical sites, in the state. There is something for almost everyone, including backpacking, camping, horseback riding, bicycling, off-road driving, fishing, and hunting.

Katy Trail State Park is designed for bicyclists and hikers. It stretches 240 miles (386 km) across the center of the state. The trail follows the route of an abandoned railroad line.

SPORTS

ENTERTAINMENT

Missouri's most famous attraction is the Gateway Arch in St. Louis. The 630-foot (192-m) monument is the tallest in the United States. Built in 1965, it is clad in shiny stainless steel. Visitors can ride a tram to an observation deck at the top.

Missouri has many amusement parks and attractions. Six Flags St. Louis and Kansas City's Worlds of Fun each have several roller coasters, dozens of other thrill rides, plus water parks.

People have fun on "Fireball," a looping thrill ride at Six Flags St. Louis.

Each year about 3 million visitors come to see the more than 18,700 wild animals at the Saint Louis Zoo.

The Saint Louis Zoo in Forest Park first opened in 1904 after the city purchased a large flight cage for birds from the World's Fair. Today, the zoo is home to more than 18,700 wild animals from 560 species. Admission is free for most exhibits.

Music has long been an important part of Missourian's lives. Kansas City played a big role in the development of jazz, while St. Louis is more well known for its blues clubs. The acclaimed St. Louis Symphony was founded in 1880. Country music is popular all over Missouri, but especially in the Ozark Mountains region. The town of Branson is a popular tourist destination because of its live music shows, museums, and theme parks.

TIMELINE

1600s-1700s—Native American tribes living in Missouri include the Illini, Missouri, Quapaw, Osage, Otoe, Sauk, Ioway, Fox, Shawnee, and Delaware.

Mid-1700s—French miners and hunters begin to settle in Missouri.

1735—Sainte Genevieve, the first permanent European settlement in Missouri, is founded.

1764—The city of St. Louis is founded.

1803—The area that will become Missouri is included in the Louisiana Purchase.

1804—Meriwether Lewis and William Clark set out with the Corps of Discovery from St. Louis to explore the West.

1812—Missouri Territory is formed.

1821—Missouri becomes the 24th state.

1861-1865—The Civil War is fought. Many battles take place in Missouri.

1904—St. Louis hosts both the Summer Olympic Games and the World's Fair. Ice cream cones are introduced. The St. Louis Zoo opens.

1914-1918—During World War I, Missouri crops are in demand to feed troops in Europe.

1929—The Great Depression begins. Many people in Missouri lose their jobs.

1941-1945—The U.S. enters World War II. Missouri sends thousands of soldiers to fight.

1965—The Gateway Arch is completed in St. Louis, Missouri.

1993—The Mississippi and Missouri Rivers flood, causing great devastation to parts of Missouri.

2014—Protests and riots break out in Ferguson after an 18-year-old African American is fatally shot by a white police officer. The National Guard is called in to restore order.

2015—The Kansas City Royals baseball team wins the World Series title.

GLOSSARY

Civil War

The war fought between the Northern and Southern states from 1861-1865. The Southern states were for slavery. They wanted to start their own country. Northern states fought against slavery and a division of the country.

Cold War

A conflict between countries because of political differences that stops short of armed warfare.

Delta

A triangular-shaped section of land formed from sediments where the mouth of a flowing river meets an ocean or other body of water. A delta can fan out over a distance of a few yards or hundreds of miles.

Fault

A break in the Earth's crust. A fault is often the site of earthquakes.

Glaciers

Huge, slow-moving sheets of ice that grow and shrink as the climate changes. During the Ice Age, some glaciers covered entire regions and measured more than one mile (1.6 km) thick.

Korean War

A war fought from 1950 to 1953 when North Korean troops invaded South Korea. The United States and other United Nations countries joined the war to help South Korea. China sided with North Korea. A truce was signed in 1953.

LEWIS AND CLARK EXPEDITION

An exploration of the West, led by Meriwether Lewis and William Clark, from 1804-1806.

LOUISIANA PURCHASE

In 1803, the United States purchased the middle section of North America from the French. The entire state of Missouri was part of the Louisiana Purchase.

OZARK MOUNTAINS

The area in the southern half of Missouri, and extending into northern Arkansas. It is heavily forested with hills, mountains, valleys, and caves.

RICHTER SCALE

A numbered scale, from 1 (low) to 9 (high), that measures the destructiveness of earthquakes. On the Richter scale, each step is 10 times stronger than the one before it. For example, an earthquake measuring 7.0 on the Richter scale is ten times greater than an earthquake measuring 6.0.

TORNADO ALLEY

An area of the United States that gets many tornadoes. Missouri is in this area because cold air from Canada meets warm air from the Gulf of Mexico, causing storms.

WORLD WAR I

A war that was fought in Europe from 1914 to 1918, involving countries around the world. The United States entered the war in April 1917.

WORLD WAR II

A conflict across the world, lasting from 1939-1945. The United States entered the war in December 1941.

INDEX